G000162390

# Take up
# Bowls

# Take up Sport

Titles in this series currently available or shortly to be published:

# Take up Bowls

Principal contributor:

**Derek Bell**

National Bowls Coach for the northern region of
England, and former British Indoor Singles Champion

assisted by

**Graham Preston**
British Crown Green Bowling Association
National Coach

SPRINGFIELD BOOKS LIMITED

Copyright © Springfield Books Limited and White Line Press 1991

ISBN 0 947655 73 5

First published 1991 by
**Springfield Books Limited**
Springfield House, Norman Road, Denby Dale, Huddersfield HD8 8TH

Edited, designed and produced by
**White Line Press**
60 Bradford Road, Stanningley, Leeds LS28 6EF

Editors: Noel Whittall and Philip Gardner
Design: Krystyna Hewitt
Diagrams: Chris Oxlade

Printed and bound in Great Britain

**Photographic credits**
Cover photograph: Supersport
Derek Bell 7, 12
Bowlers' World 51, 63
Bowls International 11
All other photographs by Noel Whittall

# Contents

# Introduction

There is a great satisfaction in sending a bowl across the ground to settle close to a distant target. Add the pleasure of doing this in friendly competition, and you have the basis of one of the most popular sports of our time. Bowls is a game which is equally suited to young or old, male or female, and all can compete on equal terms. Many disabled players enjoy the game; often blind or wheelchair-bound bowlers play alongside the able-bodied and achieve high standards of performance. Here is truly a "sport for all", so why not come along and join the converted?

*Paul Hubbal uses a Bradshaw Bowls Buggy for this demonstration match with Brian Kingdom. This specially designed wheelchair allows disabled bowlers to use both indoor and outdoor greens.*

Bowls should be within the reach of everyone, from schoolchild to pensioner, because the costs are moderate, whether on outdoor greens or in luxurious indoor stadia.

At the basic level, bowls is simply great fun, but you can also make it tremendously exciting, skilful and competitive. Whether you end up as a social bowler or a prospective champion depends on you. Whatever your choice, your new sport will give you friends and enjoyment which often last a lifetime.

Wherever we have used "he", "him" or "his" in this book, it should be taken to apply equally to players of either sex.

### Special terms

The language of bowls has developed with the game for hundreds of years, and you will probably come across some unfamiliar expressions. To help you, a glossary is provided, starting on page 61.

# What type of bowls?

In general, this book deals with flat-green bowls played on greens with full-sized rinks (see pages 19–20). This is the most popular version of the game, and it is played worldwide in countries as far apart as Canada, Australia, Japan and Argentina. However, other forms of the sport, such as *crown-green* and *short-mat* bowls, are also important, and have strong followings in certain areas. The principle of these games is basically the same as for the flat-green game, but the variations in the rules are covered in chapter 8.

---

**Measurements**
In this book we follow the governing-body rules as far as metric or imperial measurements are concerned. Therefore, when writing of the flat-green game, in which imperial measures are still commonly used, feet and inches or pounds and ounces appear first in the text, with their metric equivalents following in brackets. However, in crown-green bowls, metric measures are used for all except the weight of the bowl, so in this case the imperial equivalents are given in brackets.

---

# History of the game

Forms of a game recognisable as bowls are known to have been played as long ago as the days of the ancient Egyptians. It arrived in Britain via mainland Europe, and became so popular in the Middle Ages that it was banned by Edward III and Richard II because people were playing bowls instead of practising archery and other military skills.

In other countries the appeal of sending a ball to a target was equally attractive. In France the game of *boules* developed, in which the ball is thrown rather than rolled, while throughout Europe different versions of skittles were played. However, bowling accurately to different lengths over a smooth surface seems to have been a speciality of the British Isles.

## Developments in England

Early pictures of the game show bowls being rolled to marks or to smaller bowls called *jacks*. Games seem to have been played in a variety of directions at once, in the manner of modern crown-green bowls. The bowls used were spherical, and so would run straight. However, about the time of Henry VIII, *biased* bowls were introduced; these follow a curved path towards their objective. As you will see, bias is an essential feature of modern bowls.

Banning became a recurrent feature of the history of bowls: a statute of 1511 connected with unlawful games referred to "bowling alleys usually attached to low inns which have become the haunt of gamesters and the dissolute". A further Act, in 1541, forbade labourers, servants and the like to play "except at Christmas and then only in the master's house or presence". Others were confined to playing in their own gardens or orchards, facing a fine of six shillings and eightpence if they played elsewhere.

Henry VIII was keen enough to control his subjects' pleasure in bowls, but he made sure he had an alley built at Whitehall Palace for his own entertainment.

A century later, gambling was a big feature of the game, and one which was causing problems for royalty: it is recorded that Charles I lost £1000 to one Richard Shute, a turkey merchant from Barking, Essex.

Although the puritan government of Cromwell's England prohibited bowls as well as many other types of entertainment, we know that some forms of the game were still played, but its development in England was slow from then on.

## The Scottish developments

In Scotland the picture was far more rosy, and in the eighteenth century flat-green bowls was well on its way to becoming a national sport.

As early as 1740, superb level bowling greens were being constructed in the west of Scotland. The pioneers experimented with different types of turf, and those from the seaside gave the best results. To this day, sea-washed turf from Cumbria is still the favourite surface for British outdoor bowlers.

During this period, the Kilmarnock Bowling Club was formed. This is the oldest Scottish club and was the cradle of the modern game. Here, in 1811, a young boy called W. W. Mitchell first played bowls. Mitchell stayed with the game, and in 1849, by then a successful Glasgow advocate, he drew up the laws of bowls as then usually played in Scotland. These were adopted almost unchanged when the Scottish Bowling Association was founded in 1892. The English Bowling Association also accepted Mitchell's rules on its foundation in 1903. The EBA's first president was Dr W. G. Grace, best remembered for his outstanding feats in cricket.

A year later, in 1904, development in the British Isles was completed when Wales and Ireland formed their Associations.

## The spread of the sport

As well as gaining strength in Britain, bowls spread to British colonies and dominions throughout the world, largely during the latter half of the 19th century. It has become a national sport in Australia and New Zealand, and is very popular in Canada.

In the United States, *lawn bowling*, as it is known, has been slower to develop, even though early settlers introduced the game, and versions of it have been played there for three hundred years.

The latest country to adopt the flat-green game is Spain, where there are both grass and synthetic greens.

10

These were originally laid in areas such as the Costa del Sol to satisfy the needs of the local British communities, but now they attract large numbers of bowls enthusiasts who spend specialist holidays enjoying their sport in a climate where it rarely rains.

*Bowls clubs in Spain.*
***Top****: Cabrera, in a mountain setting*
***Above****: Calpe, on the Costa Blanca*

## The future

With the constant strengthening of international links, and the growth of the indoor game with its all-seasons appeal, bowls could well take root and thrive throughout Europe and indeed worldwide.

### The ancient game lives on

It is fortunate that there are a few historic greens dotted around England which still play to the rules and practices of the ancient game and so form a link with the past. Although the games played are similar, each club has its own rules which vary to some extent.

A typical example is what is now Barnes Bowling Club, behind the Sun Inn, where the game has been played for at least two centuries and probably far longer. Here the green is quite small, so in order to get a reasonable bowling length and a good width, play takes place diagonally, which allows two games to go on at once.

Two game versions are played. In the first, games are completed when a particular number of points is scored: 15 points with eight players, 13 points with six players, 11 points with four players, and 9 points with two players. The second version is played over 11 ends, when the scoring bowls are given different values: if more than four players are involved, the nearest bowl counts 4 points and the next three count 3, 2 and 1 respectively.

Clubs at Chesterfield, Lewes Castle, Southampton and the Tower of London are others which retain forms of the ancient game.

*The historic green behind the Sun Inn at Barnes, Middlesex*

# 3

# Equipment

## Bowls and bias

The way the bowl runs is entirely due to its shape, and not to internal weighting as is often imagined. At first sight, bowls appear to be spherical, but when you look more closely you will see that they are very carefully shaped, being slightly flattened like a Dutch cheese. They are rolled with the flattened sides vertical, and the part which contacts the ground is called the *running sole*. This is planed down more on one side than on the other, and it is this shaping which causes the bowl to run in a curve. This effect is called the *bias*.

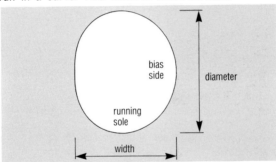

**Figure 1** Section through a typical bowl (exaggerated)

Many years ago there was a great difference in the amount of bias given to the bowls: on some of them it was so pronounced that they would almost roll in a circle on the average green. The bias of the bowls of those days was generally accepted as ranging from one, which ran almost straight, to thirteen, which had a really exaggerated curve.

For modern flat-green work, all bowls have to be within the limits of the old "bias 3". This still allows quite a variation, as you will see when you watch how different bowls run on the green.

For many years bowls were made from a very hard dense wood called lignum vitae, and they are often still referred to as "woods" by the players. However, nowadays they are made exclusively from a heavy, durable plastic material. With a few exceptions, they continue to be coloured in the traditional black or brown of the original woods.

A set of bowls is the most important item you need to purchase, so choose carefully. There is a wide variety of bowls on the market, with different weights, sizes and degrees of bias, and although as a general rule you should match the size of your bowls to the size of your hand, you need some experience before deciding which will suit you. Many retailers — particularly those based at indoor clubs — will let you try several sets before you buy. If you possibly can, get help and advice from a coach before making the final decision.

*If you can hold a bowl like this, it will probably be about the right size for you.*

### Weights and sizes of bowls

The weight of bowls tends to increase with size, but there is nothing to prevent you from using small, heavy ones or large, relatively light ones if you find they suit your style.

*There is quite a difference between the maximum and minimum sizes of bowl permitted by the rules.*

The flat-green rules allow you to use bowls with a minimum diameter of $4\frac{5}{8}$ in (118 mm) and a maximum of $5\frac{1}{8}$ in (130 mm), unless you are still using lignum vitae, in which case the upper limit is $5\frac{1}{4}$ in (133.5 mm). The full range is shown in Table 1.

**Table 1** Weights and sizes of bowls

| Size no | 0 | 1 | 2 | 3 | 4 | 5 | 6 | 7 |
|---|---|---|---|---|---|---|---|---|
| **Diameter** | | | | | | | | |
| in | $4\frac{5}{8}$ | $4\frac{3}{4}$ | $4\frac{13}{16}$ | $4\frac{7}{8}$ | $4\frac{15}{16}$ | 5 | $5\frac{1}{16}$ | $5\frac{1}{8}$ |
| mm | 118 | 121 | 122.5 | 124 | 125.5 | 127 | 128.5 | 130 |
| **Medium weight** | | | | | | | | |
| lb oz | 2 $11\frac{1}{2}$ | 2 $14\frac{1}{2}$ | 3 0 | 3 $1\frac{3}{4}$ | 3 $3\frac{3}{4}$ | 3 $5\frac{3}{4}$ | 3 6 | 3 $7\frac{3}{4}$ |
| kg | 1.24 | 1.32 | 1.36 | 1.41 | 1.47 | 1.52 | 1.53 | 1.58 |
| **Heavy weight** | | | | | | | | |
| lb oz | 2 13 | 3 0 | 3 $1\frac{3}{4}$ | 3 $3\frac{1}{2}$ | 3 $5\frac{1}{2}$ | 3 $7\frac{3}{4}$ | 3 $7\frac{3}{4}$ | 3 $7\frac{3}{4}$ |
| kg | 1.28 | 1.36 | 1.41 | 1.46 | 1.52 | 1.58 | 1.58 | 1.58 |

Although no bowl may weigh more than 3 lb $7\frac{3}{4}$ oz (1.58 kg), there are often slight variations in weight within the ranges produced by different manufacturers.

Naturally, the four bowls in your set should all be identical.

### Validity of bowls
The International Bowling Board has produced a master bowl, which has the minimum permitted bias. In each of the member countries of the IBB, the national controlling body holds a copy of this master. These are called *standard bowls*, and the bias of manufactured bowls is compared with that of the standard: none may have less bias. To certify this, each bowl is clearly stamped.

**Figure 2** The IBB stamp

**Key**
**BIB** International Bowling Board
**A** Code letter of manufacturer
**Numerals** Year of expiry
® Denotes that the stamp is a registered trade mark

National controlling bodies require bowls to carry either the IBB stamp or their own national stamp before they can be used in their competitions.

Although the minimum bias is laid down by the rules, most bowlers use more strongly biased bowls. Manufacturers produce bowls with a range of biases within the *bias 3* limits used in flat-green bowling. All bowls in a set of four should have exactly the same bias and should carry the same serial number to denote this.

---

**Buying secondhand bowls**
Quite a good saving can be made by buying bowls secondhand, but watch these points:

● It is not advisable to buy lignum vitae bowls (real wooden ones), as they need to be kept in good condition and polished regularly if they are not to dry out and even develop cracks. Although there are still some about, you don't find top bowlers using them.

● You need a matched set of bowls, so check that the serial numbers are the same on each bowl.

● Check that the date stamp is valid: having bowls tested and restamped is inconvenient, and a charge is made. Although up-to-date stamps are not normally required in club competitions and matches, once you "get the bug" you may wish to enter county and national competitions where the bowls used must have a valid stamp.

---

## Jack

The jack is a solid unbiased white ball which becomes the target for the bowlers. It is normally provided by the club or the attendant at the green.

Outdoor jacks have maximum and minimum diameters of $2^{17}/_{32}$ in (64 mm) and $2^{15}/_{32}$ in (63 mm), with maximum and minimum weights of 10 oz (283 g) and 8 oz (227 g) respectively.

Because jacks on carpets move very quickly when struck by a bowl, those used for indoor play are larger and heavier than outdoor ones:

*Diameter:* maximum $2^{21}/_{32}$ in (67 mm), minimum $2^{15}/_{32}$ in (63 mm)

*Weight:* maximum 16 oz (454 g), minimum 13½ oz (382 g)

---

## Mat

You have to stand on a mat 24 in (61 cm) long and 14 in (35.5 cm) wide when delivering the bowls. The mats are provided by the club or bowling-green attendant.

# Footwear

You will need a pair of bowls shoes as soon as you start to play: to avoid damage to the playing surface, everyone who goes onto a bowling green must wear smooth-soled heelless shoes. These come in black, brown or white, but some clubs, particularly in Britain, object to white shoes being worn, so check before you purchase.

# Dress

At county, state, national and international competitions, flat-green bowlers play in whites. The only exceptions to this are in a few televised tournaments where coloured tops are used.

Individual clubs set their own standards: some require full whites or white above the waist, while others leave it to the bowlers' choice. Whatever you wear, it should allow good freedom of movement.

Outdoor games often continue during adverse weather, so you will need waterproofs. An easy-fitting white two-piece suit is the best choice, as the white-clothing rule for most serious competitions applies to oversuits too. A good set of waterproofs will last indefinitely.

*"White above the waist" is the rule at this indoor club.*

# Measures

It is not always easy to judge by eye which bowls in a head (see chapter 12) are the scorers, so various measuring devices are used to help. Most bowlers carry a simple individual bowls measure, consisting of a tape or string, and these can solve most problems which arise during normal play.

However, umpires at important matches use a far more elaborate kit. Their range of measures includes feeler gauges, screw callipers, various long rulers and some small wedges to prevent bowls from moving during the measuring process. Official umpires are present only at special matches and tournaments, but most clubs have a full measuring kit for members to use whenever necessary.

*An umpire's comprehensive kit of measuring equipment. There are tapes, callipers, squares and even feeler gauges. The wedges are used to prevent a bowl from toppling while being measured.*

# Bowls bag

Once you have acquired your bowls, shoes, whites and waterproofs, you will need a bowls bag to carry them in. Although leather bags look good, one big enough to hold the four bowls and all your other kit will be heavy and rather expensive. Most players find that bags made of plastic or canvas materials are satisfactory: they are durable, look smart and are lighter to carry.

*Concentration at an evening league match* ➤
*on a typical outdoor green.*

# 4

# Bowling greens

## Outdoor greens

An outdoor bowling green for the flat-green game comprises a playing surface and the surrounding ditches and banks. The playing surface is usually of fine grass, although in New Zealand cotula weed is used, which provides an extremely fast and hard-wearing surface. The green is divided by threads into strips called *rinks*. From time to time, the greenkeeper will mark out the rinks in a different direction to prevent areas of excessive wear developing.

The green is surrounded by a ditch with a bank beyond. This must be able to hold the bowls without damaging them, so it usually contains a thick layer of sand.

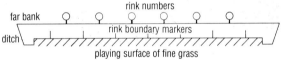

far bank — rink numbers
rink boundary markers
ditch — playing surface of fine grass

**Figure 3** Cross-section of a typical flat green

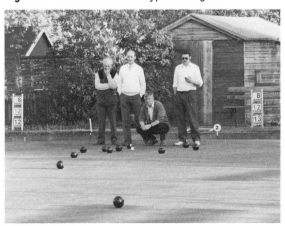

## Dimensions

**Playing area**  Maximum 44 yd (40.23 m) square, minimum 40 yd (36.58 m) square.

**Ditch**  Maximum width 15 in (381 mm), minimum 8 in (203 mm); maximum depth 8 in (203 mm), minimum 2 in (51 mm).

**Banks**  Minimum height 9 in (229 mm).

**Rinks**  Maximum width 19 ft (5.8 m), minimum 18 ft (5.5 m).

Markers are placed on each side bank to show the limits of the jack and mat positions.

*Although there is no other dress code at this club, smooth-soled, heelless shoes are essential.*

# Indoor greens

Bowls indoors is played on a carpet surface which is laid over a flat concrete bed. Layers of fibreboard and a carpet underlay provide both insulation and good playing characteristics.

Indoor greens often cover the same area as those outdoors, but some may have a playing surface only 35 yd (32 m) long and as little as 15 ft (4.57 m) wide, allowing a single rink. The banks and ditches have the same dimensions as on outdoor greens, but the rinks are not separated by boundary threads.

# 5

# The game

A bowls match consists of a series of "ends", in which the players each send their bowls towards a distant jack, attempting to leave their own bowls nearer to the jack than those of their opponents.

## Playing the game

The following sections concern the game played using International Bowling Board and World Indoor Bowling Council rules and those of their constituent bodies, which may occasionally vary slightly. The rules closely follow those originally formulated by W. W. Mitchell and revised by the Scottish Bowling Association.

### The toss
The player or team that wins the toss has the option of rolling the jack to start the first end, or of giving the jack to the other side to do so.

### Casting the jack
The player starting the game first places the mat centrally at one end of the rink, with its front edge 6 ft (1.83 m) from the ditch. With at least one foot fully on the mat, he or she then rolls the jack towards the far end of the rink. The point at which the jack comes to rest establishes the "length" of the end.

The jack must not be less than 70 ft (21.3 m) from the mat nor less than 6 ft (1.83 m) from the front ditch. There will be pegs placed on the side banks to help you judge whether the jack is short: if there is any doubt, it is measured.

Sometimes a player delivers a jack which is short, falls into the ditch or rolls out of bounds. These are called "illegal jacks". In such cases the opposition re-plays the jack but does not bowl first.

Indoor bowls governing bodies still use a minimum jack length of 75 ft (22.8 m), while the Australian Bowls Council specifies a 66 ft (20.1 m) minimum jack length.

Once the length has been checked, the jack is then placed on the centre line of the rink, level with the point where it came to rest. This is called "centring the jack"; it is done by a marker in singles matches or by the skip in team games.

*The black-and-white peg at the side of this green indicates the minimum jack length when bowling from the other end.*

In most countries the mat and the jack are centred by aligning them with the rink number, which is marked on the bank at the ends of each rink. In Australia and New Zealand the centre lines are marked on the green.

### Bowling

Once the jack is centred, the first player rolls his bowl towards it, keeping at least one foot on the mat or directly above it while making his delivery. Play continues with the players bowling alternately until the end is completed. The end score is then counted and agreed, and added to the total.

Once the first end has been played, the mat can be positioned further up the green for subsequent ends (see page 35).

To start each new end, the winner or winning team of the preceding end places the mat and rolls the jack. Each successive end is played in the opposite direction until the game is finished.

### Touchers

A bowl which touches the jack on its course up the green, either directly or after cannoning from another bowl, is called a "toucher". Because touchers remain in play ("stay live") even if they go into the ditch, they are marked with chalk to identify them when the count is made. A bowl which is knocked onto the jack is *not* a toucher.

*The two bowls on the left carry chalk crosses to show that they are touchers. Although the bowl on the right is close to the jack, it is dead and cannot score.*

### Dead bowls

Any non-toucher which goes into the ditch or rebounds from the bank and back onto the green is considered dead and must be removed.

If, during the game, a *jack* completely crosses the rink boundary line, it is dead, and the end must be replayed with the same team or bowler rolling the jack. A *bowl* which crosses the boundary line and remains completely outside it is also dead; however, one which curves over the line and comes back into your rink without touching a bowl or player in the adjacent rink remains live.

## Types of game

*Singles* is played between two opponents, each using four bowls and bowling alternately. The first to score a given number of points (normally 25) is the winner.

*Pairs* is played by teams of two players using four bowls each, over 21 ends. The first players on each side (the *leads*) play their bowls alternately, followed by the second players (the *skips*), until all 16 bowls have been played to complete each end.

*Triples* is played between two teams of three players using three bowls each. First the leads play three bowls, followed by the second players, and lastly the skips. The normal extent of a game is 18 ends.

*Fours* is generally accepted as the main game in bowls. Four players make up each team, and each player uses two bowls. The leads play their two bowls alternately, then the second players, then the third, and finally the skips. The game is played over 21 ends.

In tournaments and matches, teams or sides can be made up of any number of players, usually grouped into fours. Outdoor greens normally consist·of six rinks, so county and national teams have 24 players in six groups (also called rinks) of four. Club teams are normally smaller, usually with a maximum of 16 players.

### Sets games
Over the past few years, a sets game has been evolved with single competitors playing 3 or 5 or even 9 sets of 7-up (the first player to score 7 wins). This has developed to suit the needs of televised bowls, and has proved very popular.

As with singles, a pairs game played in sets has also been developed. The playing arrangements are the same, but the players use only two bowls each.

# Scoring

At the finish of each end, every bowl which is nearer to the jack than your opponent's nearest scores one shot (or point).

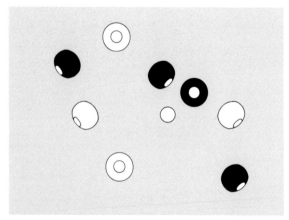

**Figure 4** In this head, black scores two shots.

After each end is played, the score and running total is noted on the score card.

Games can be won either by being the first to score a given number of shots — usually 25 in singles play — or by scoring the most shots in a particular number of ends. If an "ends" game finishes with a drawn score, an extra end is played: to start this, a coin is spun to decide who has the choice of jack.

## Measuring for shot

If there is any doubt about which bowl is nearest to the jack, a measurement is taken (see page 18).

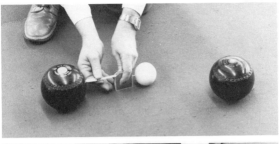

**Above** and **top**: The special measure makes it easy to check which of these two bowls is "holding shot".

*Measuring between more than two bowls*

Occasionally, the opposing nearest bowls are equidistant from the jack, and the end is therefore tied. When this happens in an ends game, the end is marked on the score card, but with each player or team scoring zero shots.

# The score card

Compliments of ⚜ **Yorkshire Bank**

HEDGELY B.C. v MAPLE B.C.

| Teams | | | Date JUNE 20th 1990 | |
|---|---|---|---|---|
| 1st D. JACKSON | | | 1st F. WARNES | |
| 2nd B. SMITH | | | 2nd G. HERRING. | |
| 3rd G. WILSON | | | 3rd A. STANDISH | |
| Skip R. THOMPSON | | | Skip H. PEARSON | |
| Ends | Score | Total | Ends | Score | Total |
| 1 | 1 | 1 | 1 | — | — |
| 2 | 2 | 3 | 2 | — | — |
| 3 | — | 3 | 3 | 3 | 3 |
| 4 | — | 3 | 4 | 1 | 4 |
| 5 | — | 3 | 5 | 1 | 5 |
| 6 | — | — | 6 | — | — |
| 7 | 2 | 5 | 7 | — | 5 |
| 8 | — | 5 | 8 | 1 | 6 |
| 9 | 3 | 8 | 9 | — | 6 |
| 10 | 2 | 10 | 10 | — | 6 |
| 11 | 1 | 11 | 11 | — | 6 |
| 12 | 1 | 12 | 12 | — | 6 |
| 13 | — | 12 | 13 | 1 | 7 |
| 14 | 2 | 14 | 14 | — | 7 |
| 15 | — | 14 | 15 | 4 | 11 |
| 16 | — | 14 | 16 | 2 | 13 |
| 17 | 1 | 15 | 17 | — | 13 |
| 18 | 1 | 16 | 18 | — | 13 |
| 19 | 2 | 18 | 19 | — | 13 |
| 20 | 1 | 19 | 20 | — | 13 |
| 21 | — | 19 | 21 | 2 | 15 |
| Total | | 19 | Total | | 15 |

R Thompson                    H Pearson.

**Figure 5** A typical score card

This example score card shows a fours game played over 21 ends between Hedgely Bowling Club and Maple Bowling Club. Hedgely score 1 shot and 2 shots at the first and second ends respectively. Maple then score a total of 5 shots; 3, 1 and 1 on the next three ends, giving a five-end total of 5 shots to 3 in Maple's favour. On the sixth end no score is recorded. This means that the end was tied. It is essential to record tied ends when scoring an ends game.

The game continues to 21 ends, with Hedgely scoring a further 16 shots to Maple's 10, making Hedgely winners by 19 shots to 15. Both skips have signed the card to show their agreement with the game result. The winning skip is then responsible for handing the card to the controlling body for the particular game.

# Duties of players

In a typical four, the players take their turns in a particular order, and each has certain duties:

*The lead* places the mat and delivers the jack according to the instructions given by the skip (see pages 46–47). He will then usually play draw shots (see chapter 7) in which his bowls will draw close to the jack and give the rest of the team a good start.

*The second* plays next. The skip may require him to place positional shots, but normally he too will draw to the head. The second also keeps the score card and ensures that the score board is kept up to date. He should check the running score with his counterpart on the other side as play progresses.

*The third* needs to be an experienced and versatile player; he directs the skip if requested, when the latter is at the other end of the green (see page 46). He also acts as measurer and agrees with his opponent the number of shots scored at each end.

*The skip* is captain of the four, as his title implies, so he is responsible for the overall tactics and strategies of the game. He introduces the players and spins a coin with his opponent to decide who is to start the game. The skip must be experienced and capable, but above all he needs to inspire confidence and to help his players to give of their best.

---

**Etiquette**

Bowls is among the friendliest of sports, and long may this continue. It has achieved this distinction largely because of the conventional rules of courtesy established and adhered to over the years. Here are some of the acts of sportsmanship which so enhance the game:

● The game is always begun with introductions, handshakes and wishes for a good game.

● Players should always stand still behind the mat or head so as not to distract a person delivering his bowl.

● Always commend a good shot, whether from a team-mate or an opponent, with a clap or a "well bowled".

● Accept flukes against you with good grace. There is a good deal of luck in bowls, but it usually evens itself out.

● End as you started, with a handshake; remember to congratulate your opponent on a game well played.

# Basic technique

Your technique involves:

● *grip:* how you hold the bowl

● *stance:* your position on the mat immediately before delivery

● *delivery action:* the complete movement from stance to the final release of the bowl

If you are new to the game, do seek the help of a qualified coach or instructor who can help you to adopt an individual style which will suit you.

## Grip

If you are to be a consistent player, the bowl must be delivered smoothly each time, without any wobble. To achieve this, it must fit comfortably into your hand.

There are basically two methods of holding a bowl when delivering: the *cradle* and *claw* grips.

With the cradle grip, the bowl is cradled in the palm of your hand with the fingers spread evenly across it. To keep the bowl steady and upright, your thumb is placed about halfway up one side, with the little finger lower on the other.

*There is no rule about which stance to choose: simply use the style that suits you.* ➤

28

When using the claw grip, your thumb and fingers support the bowl, keeping it slightly away from your palm. The bowl will be higher in your hand than when cradling it, with your thumb close to the outer rings and the little finger supporting it on the other side. The claw grip is the one most commonly used.

You can experiment with using different finger and thumb positions on both grips: many players prefer the forefinger to be placed centrally on the running face of the bowl so that it is the last point of contact at the time of release.

## Stance

The stance is the body attitude which you take up just before delivering the bowl. Styles of stance vary considerably, from fully upright to the full crouch position. Some stances are better suited to certain styles of

delivery than others, but in all of them you must be correctly positioned relative to the mat.

Law 27 requires a player to take his stance on the mat, and at the moment of delivering the jack or the bowl to have one foot wholly on or above the mat.

If a player infringes this law, he will be given one warning; further infringement will result in his bowl being declared dead.

If you wish, both feet may be on the mat, but many bowlers keep their leading foot slightly forward or even to one side.

## Styles of delivery

Your style of delivery will influence the stance you adopt. Basically, you have the choice between *athletic* and *fixed* styles.

### Athletic style

The athletic style of delivery action involves stepping forward from the mat and bending the body and knees to release the bowl smoothly in one flowing action.

*The athletic style of delivery*

You usually make a pronounced backswing as you step forwards. Most bowlers who use an athletic delivery start from a stooping or semi-crouching stance, as this means that there is less bending to do during the action than if an upright stance is adopted. Taking a full crouching stance can be very tiring, because you have to straighten your legs at the end of each delivery: the more you crouch, the more tiring the action becomes.

David Bryant, often considered to be the best bowler of all time, favours the full crouching stance coupled with an athletic delivery. He is very fit and has used this delivery for many years. You too need to be reasonably fit before you decide that this style is for you.

### Fixed style

With the fixed delivery, your body is positioned so that no further movement of the leading foot is needed and the bowl is given impetus by the arm movement. On heavy greens, or when bowling a quick delivery, it is not always easy to achieve the required power, and you will often need to impart extra impetus with a forward rocking motion of your body.

*The fixed delivery*

In spite of the slight disadvantages, many excellent bowlers use the fixed-delivery action.

With both delivery actions, a right-handed bowler leads with the left foot and vice versa.

If you watch good-class bowlers in action, you will see many variations of style, and I don't believe there is a right or wrong delivery technique, provided that the end result is a wood close to the jack! In the end, you should choose whatever style is most natural to you.

---

**Disabled players**

*Anyone* can play bowls. Do not let age or disability stop you from taking up the game, even if you do not feel that you will be able to deliver the bowl in an orthodox manner. In all cases a suitable technique can be found to enable you to achieve enjoyment and success.

---

### Forehand and backhand deliveries

The bowl will always run in a curve towards its biasing side. This side is marked by a small disc which must always face the centre line of the rink when you make a delivery. If you are right-handed and hold the bowl so that the disc is on the left, then release it on the right of the imaginary centre line, you make a *forehand* delivery. A bowl held the other way round and rolled to the left of the centre line is a *backhand* delivery. For left-handers, the opposite is the case.

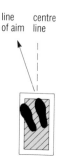

**Figure 6**
*Left* backhand delivery, and *right* forehand delivery, for a right-handed player in each case. Note the position of the feet on the mat.

## The path of the bowl

Figure 7 shows the path of a typical bowl. It appears to travel almost straight, diverging from the centre line, until it has covered about two-thirds of its distance. At this point, called the "shoulder" or "breaking point", loss of momentum causes it to move in a tighter curve towards its target.

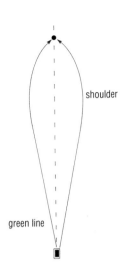

shoulder

green line

The process of a bowl travelling away from the line and then back towards it is called "taking the green". A path which follows a broad curve is said to "take a lot of green".

At first, your main task will be to get your bowls to finish on the centre line. Length will come with practice.

**Figure 7** The path of the bowl on backhand and forehand deliveries. Note the slightly different release points relative to the centre line.

## Taking aim

You aim along a straight line, although you know the bowl will curve. You first find an aiming point, bowl straight towards it along your line of aim, and allow the bowl to bend to its target. The problem for novices is how to find that aiming point ...

There are three main ways:

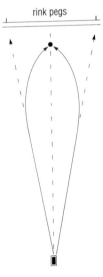

rink pegs

- Select an aiming point on the far bank, such as a boundary peg, as a guide. This is the most common method.

- Try to visualise just where the "shoulder" will be on the path of your delivery, and aim for that point. This requires more experience.

- Draw an imaginary curved green line from the jack to the mat, then deliver the bowl while visualising this line and aiming at a point about ten yards or metres along it. This is the method which I prefer.

**Figure 8** Finding an aiming point. Rink boundary pegs can be a useful guide at first.

You will soon find that you are using all sorts of extra clues to help your aim, such as patches where the grass is extra thin or of a different colour. At first you will find that aiming is rather a mystifying process, but after some practice and experience it will steadily become less of a problem. Before each game, always take advantage of the trial ends to check how broad the curve of the green line needs to be.

*A study in concentration: Mal Hughes, England Team Manager, delivers the last bowl of an end.*

A glance or two at the jack will help you to judge the impetus required to give the correct length, but you should always concentrate on your aiming point immediately before delivery.

The line of aim for long or short jacks remains the same, always provided that the green is true and the mat remains in the same place. As can be seen from Figure 9, the greater the length, the further the bowl diverges from the centre line, and the wider the shoulders become. However, the angle of delivery of the bowl is constant.

**Figure 9** The line of aim remains constant at different jack lengths.

**Grooving in**

Having decided on a suitable technique, you must cultivate and practise an error-free delivery which can be perfectly executed time and again without thought: "grooved in" as David Bryant puts it.

These points will help you:

- Visualise the curved line which the bowl will take from your hand to the target. You aim along the start of this line, which is often referred to as the *green line* or the *grass line* (see page 33).

- Make sure that your body is squarely facing along the line of aim.

- Pay attention to balance. If this is not correct from the start, you will not be able to control the delivery.

- Keep your leading foot parallel to the line, and close to it at the point of release.

- Your head should be over the line at the point of release.

- Release the bowl, hopefully without bounce or wobble, and nicely along the green line.

- After the release, your arm should follow through in the same direction as the bowl. The follow-through may be long or short, but it must be straight or you may hook the bowl.

## Factors affecting aim

### Movement of the mat

After the first end, the side playing the jack can reposition the mat if they wish. It can be moved as far as about one-third of the way up the green if need be. The distance varies according to the rules of particular governing bodies, but all greens have side-bank pegs to show the limit for mat placement. Each time the mat is moved, you will have to find new aiming points and green lines, although the angle of delivery will remain the same.

In Figure 10, with the mat moved up the rink, the angle of delivery remains the same, so the lines of aim are parallel, but the aiming points vary considerably.

**Figure 10** New aiming points are needed when the mat position changes.

When you have been playing for some time, you may find that certain lengths suit your style of bowling best, and you can try to place the mat to take advantage of this. You will find that your opponents will often move the mat as a matter of course, so the more practice you have at different lengths the better.

### Speed of the green

The way a bowl travels across the green is greatly affected by the surface: it will roll more easily on a hard, dry, close-cropped green than on a damp one with long grass.

The standard way of measuring the speed of a green is by recording the time taken for a bowl to complete its course to a jack placed 30 yd (27.4 m) from the mat. The curious result is that it will take longer to get there on a "fast" green than on a "slow" one. This is simply because it will travel much further. This sounds like a contradiction, but a glance at Figure 11 will explain it.

**Figure 11** Typical green lines on fast and slow greens

The typical fast green is hard and dry, with very short grass, and hence little friction is produced. On such surfaces bowls take a very wide path to the jack, covering a large distance at a very slow speed.

*This is a slow green, so the bowl takes a narrow line to the jack.*

The slow green may be damp and soft, with grass which is not cut short enough, so greater friction is produced. The bowl needs a lot of initial impetus but it pulls up quickly. The bias cannot take full effect, and a short narrow green line results.

The difference in speed between greens can be considerable: where cool damp conditions are prevalent, bowls may take only 9 or 10 seconds to reach the jack, whereas on hot, dry greens they may amble along for as long as 21 seconds.

The speed of the green can vary during the game, so you must be aware of this and adjust your delivery accordingly.

### Movement of the jack

Although the jack starts each end on the centre line, it can easily be knocked off it during the course of play. Obviously you have to adjust your aiming procedures when this happens.

The best way is to regard the imaginary line from the mat to the new jack position as the centre line, and to adjust your aiming point and stance on the mat accordingly.

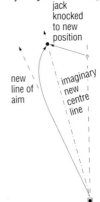

**Figure 12** Coping with an off-centre jack

### Surface variations

Bowling greens are rarely absolutely flat and true, so your bowl will often cross a hollow or a hump. Coupled with the effect of the bias, this will affect its course, causing it either to straighten or to swing more violently. Sometimes this effect can be used to advantage, but most players try to avoid problem areas by changing the mat position or jack length as soon as there is an opportunity to do so.

### Windy conditions

Windy conditions are the most difficult to deal with, especially on fast greens, where the bowl can be blown a long way off course.

● *Strong cross-winds:* If the wind is strong and consistent, I normally prefer the bowl to curve into the wind during the second part of its run, and choose a forehand or backhand delivery accordingly. This reduces the bias effect overall, and a very narrow green line, sometimes almost straight, can be achieved. Obviously, if the wind drops while the bowl is running, the bias takes effect and the bowl is wasted.

- *Light cross-winds:* In light or intermittent winds I tend to use the hand that will take the bowl into the wind on the first part of its run, allowing its natural bias (assisted by the wind) to bring it back to the centre line.

- *Head and tail winds:* These do not affect your aim very much, but they do make it very difficult to get the correct length. Practice and patience are essential.

---

**Mastering the art**

Bowls is an art and not a science, so it is impossible always to be perfect with your aim. Attention to these points will help:

- Establish an aiming procedure to suit you.

- Concentrate on the aiming point and line of aim.

- Try to develop a good, "grooved in" delivery along the line of aim.

- Learn from your last bowl, correcting your line where necessary. Remember that every bowl delivered will teach you something about the rink you are playing on.

- Do not try to follow the line of an opposite-handed player: because his bowl will be released at a different point on the green, it will take a different line to the jack.

---

## Finding the length

Getting good length is the most difficult part of all bowling games. Most players can achieve an accurate line fairly consistently, but if you can regularly add the crucial ingredient of good length, you will soon be a winner.

Unlike *taking the green* (see page 63), bowling to length cannot readily be taught, although a coach can offer useful help and advice. The main way to improve is to practise, practise and practise again.

Playing competitive games and enjoying "roll-ups" (casual friendly games) can be very helpful in developing a feeling for length, but you also need to practise regularly on your own or with a partner. Simply drawing to a jack with four bowls end after end can be boring, so you need to devise tasks which will keep you interested. I like to divide these practices into three sections:

## Section one

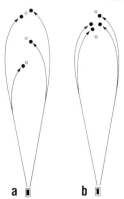

**a** Set three jacks on the centre line at intervals of 2 or 3 yards apart. Practise drawing to each jack in any order.

**b** Set two jacks on the centre line about 2 yards apart, depending on the level of difficulty required, and attempt to group all four bowls between the jacks.

**Figure 13**

**c** Set four jacks in a square and draw four bowls into the square. Your bowls may pass either inside or outside the nearer pair of jacks.

**d** Draw to the jack around two bowls placed in front of it.

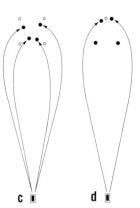

Always practise both forehand and backhand deliveries in all cases.

## Section two

Practise bowling to jacks of different lengths on successive ends, using different mat positions. Many people simply place the jack in position for this type of exercise, but I prefer to roll the jack even though walking down to centre it is a bit of a chore when on your own. The advantage is that it helps you to get a "feel" for its length.

## Section three

If you have a partner, finish the session with a few ends of competitive bowls. In singles play, you will usually be bowling for length, but it is also a good idea to make a few weighted deliveries too (see chapter 7). Always concentrate throughout the session, and try to end each part on a high — it's good for morale.

# Correcting length

To give the correct impetus to the bowl in order to achieve the required length involves a balance of body and arm movement; adjusting your delivery to alter the length bowled by a very small distance requires almost imperceptible changes.

Rather than thinking consciously about changing the length of step, backswing and follow-through, you will probably find it more helpful to think in terms of speed of delivery. For example, when a player is constantly bowling heavily (too fast) during my coaching sessions I tend to lower my voice and tell him to s-l-o-w i-t d-o-w-n a little. This usually produces the desired effect after a little practice.

*Regular practice and coaching sessions like this are the best ways to improve length as well as smoothness of delivery.*

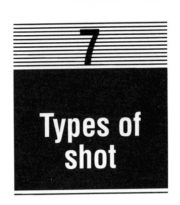

# Types of shot

## The draw shot

The draw shot is one which is delivered with just the right aim and length for it to stop very close to the target — usually the jack. This is called "drawing" to the jack. As the aim of the game is to get as many bowls as possible close to the jack, it is the most important shot in the game. You should devote most of your practice time to perfecting this shot.

*A bowl with correct line and length draws to the jack.*

# Variations of the draw shot

In all the following diagrams, it is assumed that a right-handed player has made the delivery.

### The rest shot

This is similar to the normal draw shot, except that the object is for the bowl to end up actually resting against its target.

**Figure 14** The rest shot

### The positional draw

You often want to position a bowl at the rear of the head to cover it in case the jack is moved. This is when you use the draw technique to make the bowl finish up in a particular place rather than close to another object.

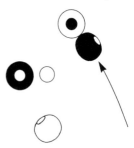

**Figure 15** The positional draw. Black has drawn on the forehand to cover the rear white bowl in case the jack is moved during the course of the end.

### The block shot

You will often want to leave your bowl in such a position that it blocks your opponent's path to the jack. This is achieved by using the basic draw as a blocking shot.

**Figure 16** The block shot. Here black has drawn an excellent shot so, using either hand, he now draws a short bowl to the centre line as a blocker. This will protect his own shot bowl if his opponent attempts to drive. A blocker like this should be at least five or six feet short, otherwise it may be driven onto the jack.

### The wick shot

Your bowl "wicks off" another when it touches it lightly and moves away at a shallow angle. This effect, used with care, can often take your bowl past the opposition and deep into the head.

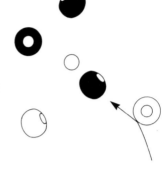

**Figure 17** The wick shot. Black has bowled a forehand delivery which then "wicks off" the white bowl to bring it close to the jack.

## Weighted shots

Any shot which is delivered with more power than would be needed for a simple draw is a *weighted* shot. These are used to move other bowls in the head, and the power is adjusted accordingly. If you are just trying to nudge the jack slightly nearer to an existing bowl, your weighted delivery may be little more than a draw shot; at the other extreme, you may be trying to take the jack into the ditch with the all-out *drive*, or *firing shot*.

At the more than a draw shot; at the other extreme, you may be trying to take
the jack into the ditch with the all-out *drive*, or *firing
shot*.

When playing with weight, always size up the head carefully, and choose the hand which will give you the best chance of achieving the shot. Remember that the more weight you use, the straighter is the path of your bowl, so your aim must be adjusted carefully.

### The trail shot

The object of the trail shot is to move the jack to a more favourable position.

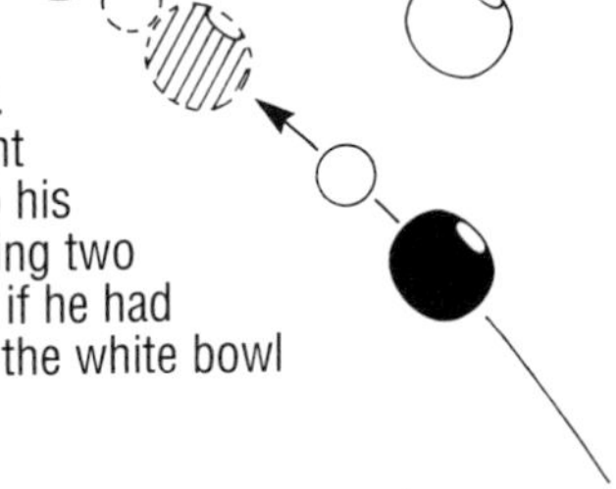

**Figure 18** The trail shot. Black plays with sufficient weight to trail the jack to his existing back bowl, scoring two shots. In this case, even if he had failed, he might have hit the white bowl and so gained one shot.

### The yard-on shot

In this shot the aim is to move an opponent's bowl a short distance away from a scoring position. You deliver your bowl with enough weight to take it about a yard past the jack if it does not hit another bowl on the way.

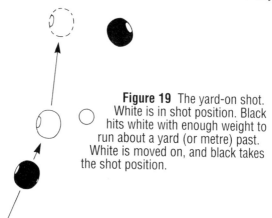

**Figure 19** The yard-on shot. White is in shot position. Black hits white with enough weight to run about a yard (or metre) past. White is moved on, and black takes the shot position.

### The running shot

The running shot uses more power than the yard-on, and naturally is used to move the opposing bowl over greater distances.

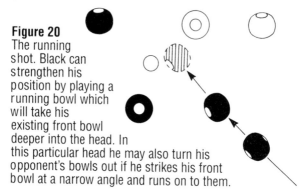

**Figure 20**
The running shot. Black can strengthen his position by playing a running bowl which will take his existing front bowl deeper into the head. In this particular head he may also turn his opponent's bowls out if he strikes his front bowl at a narrow angle and runs on to them.

### The drive

The drive is often called the *firing shot* or the *strike*. It is the most powerful shot in bowls. This is the shot which takes the jack right off the green and into the ditch — and sometimes other bowls too. The drive is often used by a losing player to "kill" an end when he can see no way of retrieving the situation as the head develops.

Most bowlers aim at a point alongside the target when driving, remembering that a relatively small amount of bias will take effect. With short jacks, or on very fast greens where there is little friction, it is possible for energetic players to aim almost straight at the target.

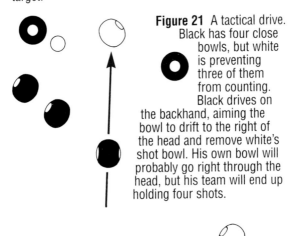

**Figure 21** A tactical drive. Black has four close bowls, but white is preventing three of them from counting. Black drives on the backhand, aiming the bowl to drift to the right of the head and remove white's shot bowl. His own bowl will probably go right through the head, but his team will end up holding four shots.

**Figure 22** A desperation drive. Black is in the unenviable position of being four shots down, and has little chance of drawing to the jack with his last delivery. He decides to drive, in the hope that he will either improve his position in the head — after all, it cannot be worse — or knock the jack off the rink, so making the end dead. He can choose to use either a forehand or a backhand delivery.

---

**Don't overdo it**
When driving, the object is to release your bowl as fast as you can while retaining accuracy and balance. If you miss the target your bowl will be wasted, or may even cause damage to your own position, so don't drive or "fire" indiscriminately — *use the drive shot sparingly.*

# Shot selection

Heads of bowls are like fingerprints — no two are the same. Selecting the correct shot to play is thus a skill which can come only with experience. However, there are certain guidelines which will help:

● The bowler who puts most bowls into the head wins most games, so skill at drawing to the jack is most important.

● It pays to have a bowl past the head (see the positional draw, page 42).

● Try not to lose more than one shot at any end.

● The drive shot can be risky, so consider the state of the game carefully before using it.

● Block shots are difficult to get right, and so are rarely effective. You can easily end up blocking your own shots. Use blocks sparingly, if ever.

# Instructions on the rink

Playing the game of bowls successfully is often dependent upon instructions shouted from a skip or partner at the other end of the green. This has led to the development of a number of stock phrases:

**Can you see it?** Do you think there's a way through the head for your bowl to find the jack or a target bowl?

**Ditch it!** Hit the jack sufficiently hard to force it into the ditch.

**Get them up; be up reach; you're short — put a bit on** Terms of displeasure! Your bowls are not reaching the head, and short bowls are a nuisance because they will block the way to the jack.

**Jack high** Your bowl has come to rest level with the jack.

**Kill it** or **hit it** Use a firing shot to destroy the head or make the end dead.

**Put a yard on** A yard of extra length is needed.

**Take this bowl out** Play with sufficient weight to remove a particular bowl from the head.

**Turn this bowl in** Play with sufficient weight to turn the indicated bowl nearer to the jack.

**You're heavy — take a bit off** Your bowl has passed the target.

**You're tight** or **you're narrow** You haven't given the bowl sufficient green.

**You're too wide** You have given the bowl too much green.

Whenever you are calling instructions, always be positive. A bowler always knows when he's bowled a bad bowl, and nobody does it on purpose. "Increase your weight by a yard" is better than "You're a yard short". Positive instructions in the right tone of voice can be a great help to your team-mate.

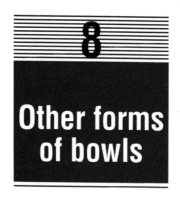

# 8

# Other forms of bowls

## CROWN-GREEN BOWLS

Crown-green bowls is an important though localised form of the sport which is played largely in the midland and northern counties of England, in North Wales and in the Isle of Man. As the name suggests, the game is played on greens which rise to a shallow but distinct hump, usually in the centre.

Although experiments have been made, it has proved extremely difficult to build satisfactory indoor greens with crowns, so this form of bowls remains essentially an outdoor game. The only indoor crown green at present in existence adjoins the Tranmere Rovers Football Club ground in Birkenhead, Merseyside.

Although most crown-green bowls clubs are entirely amateur, there is a long tradition of professional play and modest betting associated with the game.

## The crown greens

When a new green is being made, the British Crown Green Bowling Association (BCGBA) recommends an area of 37 m x 37 m (121 ft x 121 ft) with a crown 300–375 mm (12–15 in) high. This allows for four singles or pairs games to be played at the same time. However, crown greens vary to a great extent and no two are identical. They can be square, oblong, round, or even completely irregular in plan, but all are surrounded by a ditch.

**Figure 23** An exaggerated section through a typical crown green. Some greens have more than one crown.

Although a single crown is normal, there are many variations: some greens have several crowns, or wide slopes rising to ridges, while others are almost flat. Sometimes it seems that the only thing they all have in common is that they are large enough to allow the jack to be bowled or cast to the required minimum length of 19 metres (62 ft 4 in).

# Crown-green equipment

### Bowls

Crown-green bowlers generally use smaller, lighter bowls than their flat-green counterparts. This is because it requires a good deal of strength to bowl from corner to corner on a large crown green — distances of 50 m (165 ft) or more are possible. This takes far more effort than the maximum length of 36 yd (32.9 m) achieved on a finely manicured flat green. Curiously, the BCGBA do not specify any weights or sizes for the bowls that are used in the game.

Bowls of 2 bias full are the most commonly used, though some bowlers prefer them to have slightly stronger bias than this. "2 bias full" means that the amount of bias is right at the top of the range allowed within the bias 2 limits (see page 13). Weights vary from 2 lb 4 oz (1.02 kg) to 3 lb (1.36 kg), increasing usually in 2 oz (57 g) intervals. The 2 lb 10 oz (1.19 kg) bowl is probably the most popular; it is about the equivalent of a size 3 flat-green bowl (see Table 1 on page 15).

### Jack

Although there are no rules about the sizes of bowls, the requirements for crown-green jacks are quite specific. They can be either black with white mounts and spots, or white with black mounts and spots. The spots are on the non-bias side, and show clearly which "peg" your opponent is using. Since October 1987, all jacks stamped by the British Crown Green Bowling Association and the British Parks Bowling Association have minimum and maximum weights of 595 g (1 lb 5 oz) and 680 g (1 lb 8 oz) respectively. The previous limits were slightly lighter, and many of these older jacks are still in use. Standard jacks are of 2 bias full, and their diameter must be between 95 mm (3.74 in) and 98 mm (3.86 in).

### Footer

The mat is called a footer in the crown-green game. It is much smaller than those used in flat-green, being a disc between 128 mm (5 in) and 154 mm (6 in) in diameter.

### Measuring

Other items of equipment, including measures, are the same as those used in the flat-green game. However, when measuring in crown-green bowls, the convention is for two persons to take part; in flat-green this only happens when the distance is inconvenient for one measurer.

# The game

The object of the game and the method of scoring are just the same as in flat-green bowls, but there are also some significant differences, the most obvious of which concerns the jack. Crown-green bowls is played with a biased jack which is larger than its flat-green counterpart and which looks like a small bowl. Players often have their own jacks which they use in practice or roll-ups. However, in competitions, clubs issue players with standard jacks. The point at which the jack stops at the beginning of an end is always referred to as a "mark".

The other main difference is that you are not confined to rinks: in crown-green bowls you can bowl in any direction and use the whole of the green. It is quite usual to play diagonally across the green, and you will often see bowls from different ends crossing in the centre.

### Crown-green deliveries

Crown-green bowlers adopt an upright stance and use an athletic delivery action (see page 30). The crouch or semi-crouch positions are not used. The upright position also helps the bowler to have a clear view of the path to be followed to the jack. To bowl 60 metres (200 ft) on a wet, heavy green takes quite a lot of energy, so many players step out a little further to develop the power to reach a long mark.

### Singles

The mat, usually called a *footer* in crown bowls, is placed within 3 m (9 ft 10 in) of the entrance to the green and 1 m (3 ft 3 in) from the ditch. The leading player takes up a position on the footer and casts the jack in any suitable direction. Assuming that the jack travels for at least the minimum legitimate length of 19 metres (62 ft 4 in), the leading player follows it with his first bowl, aiming to find the same line and length.

Before casting the jack, you must indicate clearly which hand you are to bowl when the delivery is made ("finger or thumb peg"). Your back foot must be in contact with the mat at the moment of release, so if you are right-handed, you must place your right toe on the footer and step forward with your left foot as you deliver. For left-handers the opposite applies. Exceptions to this rule may be made for people with physical disabilities.

If you are playing second, you must watch the jack and your opponent's bowl very carefully to ascertain which line you need to take before bowling your first bowl. When each player has bowled two bowls, the end is complete and the score is counted.

After each end is concluded, the last player carries the footer to the jack. The winner of the end bowls the next jack; he may move the footer provided it remains within a metre (3 ft 3 in) of the old jack position. The playing of ends continues, and in friendly and club games the first player reaching a score of 21 shots is the winner. In many large competitions, games of 31-up are played.

*Phil Owen casts the jack diagonally during a Henselite British Crown Green Individual Merit competition.*

### Pairs

The first player of the pair is called the lead and the second player is the skip. Each player delivers two bowls per end: when the leads have played their two bowls alternately, the skips repeat the process until the end is complete. As with singles, pairs games are usually played to a score of 21.

### Basic rules

Here are the basics which beginners need to know on their first introduction to the game:

● If the jack is driven into the ditch during the course of play, the end is deemed dead, with neither player scoring. Play is restarted with the footer on the green one metre (3 ft 3 in) in from where the jack left the green. The player who originally started the end restarts it.

- If the jack is displaced by a bowl or jack from another game, it may be replaced if all the players agree; otherwise the end is void.

- If the jack is impeded on its way to a mark, it must be returned and replayed.

- If the jack comes to rest on a mark close to another jack, the last one to stop must be returned.

- When a running bowl is impeded by a player from another game, or by any other external cause, it must be returned and replayed. If this happens to the leader's first bowl, he may if he wishes have the jack returned and set another mark.

- If the jack is bowled short or off the green, the opponent sets the mark from the same mat position. The initial player still bowls the first bowl.

- If a bowler plays out of turn, the bowl is returned and played in the correct order.

- If a player delivers a wood other than his own, it is deemed dead and the player forfeits a bowl. The bowl is returned to its owner to be played.

- When a player bowls to block an opponent's course, if the bowl travels less than three metres (9 ft 10 in) it will be removed from the green.

## ENGLISH BOWLING FEDERATION BOWLS

You will find bowls played under English Bowling Federation (EBF) rules only in the midland and eastern regions of England. The EBF is not affiliated to the International Bowling Board. The game is basically an outdoor flat-green game with rules which vary from those of the IBB in the following ways:

- To start the game the mat is placed 6 ft (1.83 m) from the ditch, but subsequently it may be placed anywhere up to 12 ft (3.65 m) in.

- The jack remains live if played into the ditch. However, "touchers" are not a feature of the game, so bowls in the ditch are accounted dead.

- Only bowls which are 6 ft (1.83 m) or less from the jack may be counted as scorers.

- A bowl on the string between the rinks is dead.

- The game may be played as two- or four-bowl singles, two-bowl triples or two-bowl mixed pairs.

- Players in pairs or triples may change positions at the conclusion of any end.

EBF bowls had its origins when the Midlands and East Anglian Bowling Association was formed in 1926 to promote a three-a-side game using two bowls per player as distinct from the EBA practice of four bowls. In 1945 the name of the Association was changed to the English Bowling Federation, and it then included nine county members from the Midlands, North East and East Anglian areas of England. The Federation has grown steadily since then, and many clubs within its area are affiliated to both the EBF and the EBA.

## INDOOR BOWLS

## Short-mat bowls

Short-mat bowls is played in club rooms and halls throughout the UK, the Isle of Man and many parts of Australia. Recently it has become established in Belgium, and is expected to spread throughout Europe. The potential for growth is great, as only limited space is required and so existing halls can be used.

The rink mat is the carpet on which the sport takes place. It has maximum and minimum lengths of 45 ft (13.7 m) and 40 ft (12.2 m) respectively, and its width is 6 ft (1.83 m) with a 2 in (50 mm) tolerance. It must be green in colour and have a suitable underlay or an approved bonded backing.

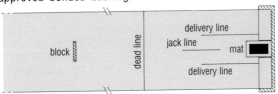

**Figure 24** The standard markings for short-mat bowls

A wooden fender is placed at each end of the rink mat, allowing for a ditch area 12 in (300 mm) wide. The fender serves the same purpose as the bank in the flat-green game.

Placed in the centre of the rink mat is a wooden block 15 in (450 mm) long. This is to prevent the drive or firing shot being used. The drive would be too easy to play over the relatively short distances involved, and it would be potentially dangerous to people and property in confined areas. However, it is legitimate to deliver weighted or running bowls, but lots of skill and judgement are needed to allow them to pass the block and to curve into the head. As in all other forms of bowls, the draw shot is the most important of all.

Short-mat bowls is played to almost the same rules as flat-green bowls, using the same equipment. However, there are some essential differences:

● The mat is always placed between the mat delivery lines, with a short end touching the fender.

● The jack is placed on the jack line in a position chosen by the player or team commencing the end.

● At the point of delivery, the front foot must be within the delivery lines.

● Bowls which come to rest in the dead area, touch the block, go over the block, or leave the rink mat, are accounted dead and must be removed.

The short-mat game is organised in an association of clubs. The governing body in England is the English Short Mat Bowling Association, which holds its own national championships. The game is organised on similar lines in the rest of the British Isles, Australia and Belgium.

# Carpet bowls

Carpet bowls is very similar to short-mat bowls, but is played on an even smaller rink mat, normally 30 ft (9.1 m) by 6 ft (1.83 m) with smaller bowls and jack.

As in short-mat bowls, a barrier is placed midway along the direct path to the jack, but there are no ditch areas or fenders, and players do not use delivery mats.

When delivering, you stand just off the end of the rink mat, with one foot on either side of the centre line. It is a foot fault if you let either foot touch the mat, or be more than twelve inches (30 cm) wide of the centre line.

### Removing the jack

Carpet bowls is a game where you have to control the force of your deliveries very carefully. If you hit the jack hard enough to take it off the rink, your team will be penalised. The penalty increases according to which player removes the jack: one shot is deducted if the lead plays the jack out of bounds, two if the second offends, and so on, up to four shots if the fourth player or skip defaults.

In spite of these quite severe penalties, situations can arise when it is worthwhile to kill the end by removing a jack from the rink. For example, if a skip is five shots against, with little or no chance of improving the position, he may try to hit the jack out of play, thereby only losing four shots.

# 9

# Bowls coaching

Informal coaching has been going on in bowls probably since the game began, with beginners looking to the "old hands" to help them with delivery techniques, game tactics and strategies. Organised coaching is a fairly recent innovation, but is now firmly established in Australia, New Zealand and the British Isles.

The English Bowls Coaching Scheme is a good example of the modern approach. Since its inception in 1979, it has developed a network of 30 advanced coaches, over 700 coaches and about 4000 instructors, all holding qualifications issued under the scheme. Most counties have a county coach, and a large number of clubs have at least one instructor.

The scheme is funded by the Sports Council and by donations from all the controlling bodies of bowls, including the crown-green and EBF versions, so all bowlers are encouraged to benefit from it. Almost all clubs offer beginners' courses of up to five 2-hour sessions.

From the start, a good coach will help you to develop a delivery technique which builds on your own natural movement. You will gradually be introduced to exercises which develop good line and length bowling while encouraging an error-free style. After one or two sessions, you will be introduced to the game itself.

*A video coaching session to spot faults in delivery*

# 10

# Bowls clubs

Although you can play bowls on a casual basis by going to public greens, you will get the fullest enjoyment from the game when you join a club.

## Outdoor clubs

Outdoor clubs are generally one of two types — private clubs, where the green is owned and tended by the club, or public-green clubs, which use facilities provided by a local authority.

Most clubs will require you to be proposed for membership by two existing members. Don't let this put you off — if you go along to the green and chat with the players, you will soon find yourself being welcomed and introduced to the club secretary.

### Private clubs

A member of a private club pays an annual subscription which helps to cover green and clubhouse maintenance, plus administration costs.

*A private club with its clubhouse almost on the green*

Many private clubs have a licensed bar which acts as a base for social functions and generates the extra funds which always seem to be needed.

### Public-green clubs

Many clubs operate from municipal greens which are also open to members of the general public. The usual system is for one or two rinks to be set aside for casual players to use on payment of a rink fee, normally based on an hourly rate, while the rest are reserved for the club during matches or competitions.

As the local authority maintains the green, members pay only a small club subscription to cover administration costs for the year, but they pay their own rink fees each time they play. Many councils now offer season tickets which give worthwhile savings. The social functions of public-green clubs are often held in outside premises, as the council usually provides only a small pavilion by the green.

Looking to the future, it is as well to join a club which is affiliated to your regional or national organisation, so that as your skill improves you can enter competitions controlled by these bodies. In the meantime, enter the club competitions: they are great fun, and you will learn a lot from them.

## Indoor clubs

Indoor stadia are altogether more expensive to build, maintain and administer than outdoor greens. Initial finance for the building of these premises can come from many different sources: private individuals, existing large outdoor clubs, councils, or even supermarkets.

*An indoor club allows comfortable shirtsleeve bowling throughout the year.*

The Hartlepool Club, scene of many of the photographs in this book, was built by the Borough of Hartlepool in Cleveland. It is leased to the Hartlepool and District Indoor Bowls Club, which is responsible for paying rent and rates and for the everyday management. In this way it has become a private club run by bowlers for bowlers.

There are not many indoor clubs to choose from in the UK, and they are fairly well scattered, so most bowlers simply join the nearest one. If you are lucky enough to be within striking distance of an indoor club, you will be able to play bowls all the year round.

Because of the popularity and relative scarcity of indoor clubs, you may find that there are waiting lists for membership.

## Session play

So that indoor greens can cater for large numbers of members, games at club level are generally organised on a time basis. Usually the hall is open for twelve hours a day, and this is divided into six sessions of two hours each. This amount of time does not allow full pairs, triples or fours games to be completed, so "domestic" rules are devised to make the games fit the sessions. Games of 16 ends are popular, while in some clubs they simply play to a time limit, with the end of the session signalling the completion of the game.

Because most clubs are heavily committed to domestic league play, you will find that specific sessions are allocated each day for practice.

# How the sport is run

## National organisation

Outdoor bowls clubs are usually affiliated to the national governing body via county, state or regional organisations. In almost all cases the male and female games are controlled separately.

Indoor clubs tend to be affiliated directly to the national body, without regional involvement.

National bodies hold their championships annually, when county, state or regional champions, both individual and team, meet to compete for national honours.

## Bowls in Britain

The four countries of the United Kingdom also join together under the auspices of the British Isles Bowls Council and the British Isles Indoor Bowls Council, with separate councils for women.

These bodies organise annual home international team and individual championships, playing in each of the four countries in turn.

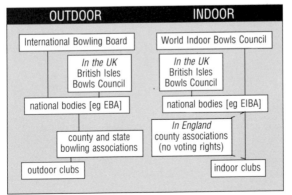

**Figure 25** The structure of the sport

It is interesting to note that, for World Championship events, Northern Ireland and Eire join together in sending players to form the Irish team.

# World bowls

At world level, the outdoor game is controlled by the International Bowling Board and the International Women's Bowling Board. These bodies organise world championships at which five players from each affiliated country play in singles, pairs, triples and fours championships, plus the overall five-person team championship. These events take place every four years.

At present the IBB has ten full members, fourteen associate members and four affiliated members.

The World Indoor Bowls Council is a much smaller organisation, with seven members at the time of writing, although future growth is assured.

# Commonwealth Games

A joint committee of the IBB and the IWBB acts for the Commonwealth Games Federation to organise bowling for this event, which takes place every four years.

# Bowling terms

**Cast** The act of rolling the *jack* at the start of an *end*.

**Draw** A shot which is delivered with just enough *weight* to stop at the required point — usually close to the jack; hence the expression "drawing to the jack".

**Drive** A powerful shot designed to break up the head and possibly take the jack and other bowls off the green: also called a *firing shot* or a *strike*.

**End** Each time the players have all delivered their bowls towards the jack, they are said to have completed an end.

**Finger peg** The crown-green expression for a forehand delivery.

**Firing shot** Another name for the *drive*.

**Footer** The rubber mat used in crown-green bowls.

**Hand** A bowls delivery may be either forehand or backhand. Bowls are clearly marked with a small disc on their *biasing* side; this is the side to which they will curve when rolling. A forehand delivery is made with the disc close to the player's little finger. On a backhand delivery, the thumb will be close. You should always "play the hand" which gives your bowl the clearest run to the jack. See also *peg*.

**Head** The arrangement of bowls which group around the jack as play proceeds during each *end*.

**Jack** This may be called kitty, cot or white. "Cot" is used in East Anglia, and is said to derive from the charitable efforts of bowlers in that area. After the match bowlers would test their skills at drawing to the jack. Part of the proceeds of the wager were given to the local cottage hospital, hence the word "cot". You still hear the challenge "a penny on the cot".

**Jack high** A bowl which comes to rest with its nearest point level with the nearest point of the jack, when viewed in relation to the front edge of the mat.

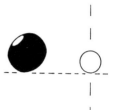

**Lead** The first player in each team to deliver his bowl during an end.

**Mark** The point at which the jack comes to rest in crown-green bowls.

**Marker**

**1** A mark on the side of the green to indicate the centre line of the rink or the limit of the mat position.

**2** A match official who checks the bowls, keeps the score, marks *touchers*, signals whether a bowl is *jack high*, measures doubtful shots and generally oversees the conduct of a game. The marker is responsible to the umpire.

**Mitchell** Another name for a *toucher*, commonly heard in Scotland. It is named after W. W. Mitchell, who drew up the first rules of the modern game.

**Peg** Term used in connection with the direction the bowl will curve when delivered. For example, if it is held so that the bias will take it to the left, the bowler is said to be "using the left peg".

**Plant** Bowls which are so positioned that by striking one, another is moved in the desired direction. Also called a *set*.

**Rest** A bowl which remains in contact with another bowl or the jack is said to *rest* it.

**Rink**

**1** The group of bowlers playing an end constitutes a rink.

**2** The division of the green upon which a single game is played. Mitchell's original rules use the word in both senses. The term came from the game of curling, which is similar to bowls on ice.

**Set** see *plant*.

**Shot bowl** The bowl nearest to the jack in the head.

**Skip** The skipper of a team: he plays last in each end.

**Strike** The crown-green equivalent of the *drive* and the *firing shot*.

**Taking the green** The way a bowl rolls away from its target and then curves towards it is called *taking the green*. A slow shot with a highly biased bowl will "take a lot of green".

**Thumb peg** The crown-green expression for a backhand delivery.

**Toucher** A bowl which touches the jack when played, but ends up in the ditch. Also called a *Mitchell*.

**Weight** A weighted bowl is one which is delivered with power and speed.

*Something to aim for: the final of the Waterloo Handicap at Blackpool, the star event of crown-green bowls.*

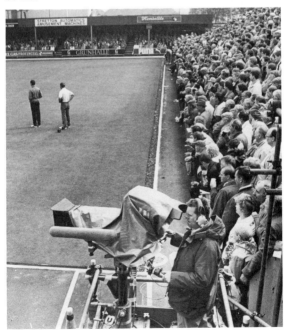

# Useful addresses

## British Isles

British Isles Bowling Council
c/o 43 Belfast Road
Ballynure, Ballyclare
Co Antrim  BT39 9TZ

British Isles Women's Bowling
Council
c/o Carracombe, The Clays
Market Lavington
Wiltshire SN10 4AY

British Crown Green Bowling
Association
c/o 14 Leighton Avenue
Maghull
Liverpool  L31 0AH

English Bowling Federation
c/o 62 Frampton Place
Boston
Lincolnshire
PE21 8EL

British Isles Indoor Bowls Council
c/o 8/2 Backdean
Ravelston Terrace
Edinburgh  EH4 3EF

British Isles Women's Indoor
Bowls Council
c/o 16 Windsor Crescent
Radyr
Cardiff  CF4 8AE

## Overseas

American Lawn Bowling
Association
c/o 8710 Tern Avenue
Fountain Valley
California 92708

Australian Bowls Council
c/o Box Q 293
Queen Victoria PO
Sydney, NSW 2000

Canadian Lawn Bowling Council
1600 James Naismith Drive
Gloucester
Ontario
K1B 5N4

New Zealand Bowling Association
c/o PO Box 17–215
Greenlane
Auckland 5

## International

International Bowling Board
EBA Headquarters
Lyndhurst Road
Worthing
West Sussex
England
BN11 2AZ

International Women's Bowling
Board
c/o 78 River Bend Avenue
Napier, New Zealand

World Indoor Bowls Council
c/o 44 Stamford Road
Bournemouth, Dorset  BH6 5DS